Made in the USA
Coppell, TX
31 October 2020

40556902R00056